Their Own

Dylan Lucero

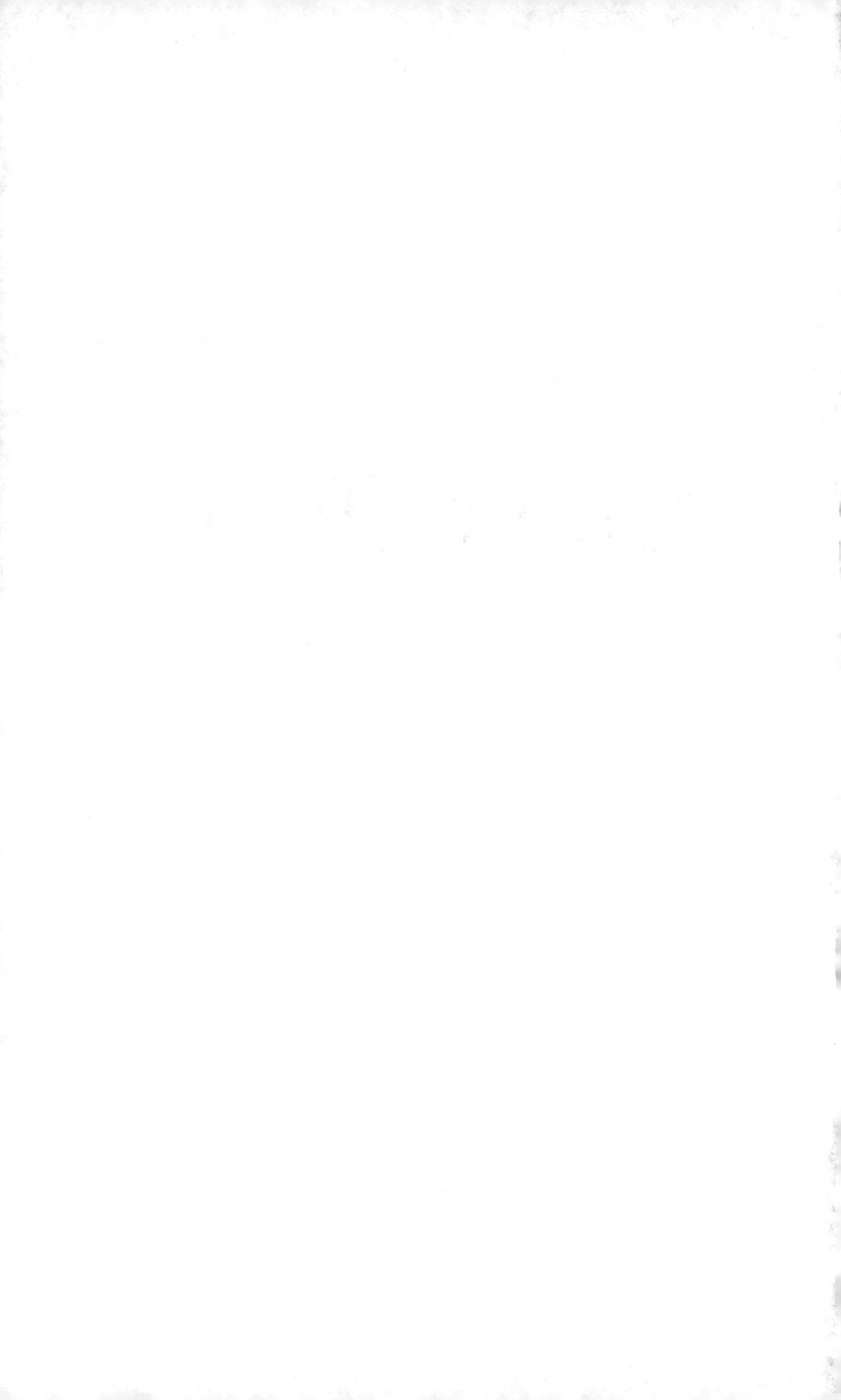

Author's Note

I dedicate this work to my friends and family, immediate and distant. Thank you for being a part of my life and supporting me through all these years. You are everything I'm thankful for.

I would also like to acknowledge the dear reader who has found their way to this book. No matter when you happen to read it, I hope that the passion I've poured into it may resonate with you.

1 Dylan Lucero

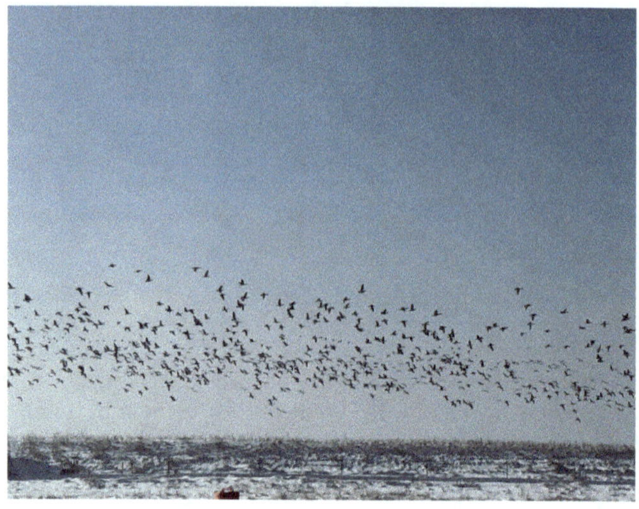

As the morning gleams
you wake up just to see
nothing is as it seems
so you get lost inside your dream
words on a phone and on TV
Streaming now are the movie scenes
a morning lost as it’s lost its gleam
dignity lost to a computer screen

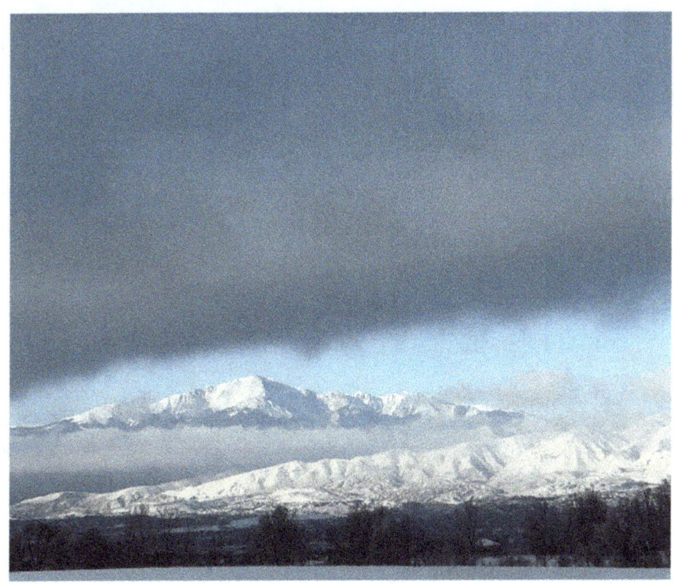

Winter is ending,
yet it feels like it just began
I can't even see the mountains
when the fog begins to land

Everyone hides inside
Everything stowed for the coming weeks
Maybe months,
maybe years

The beginning of spring
postponed for now
Guess I'll give myself time
to form my own plan

3 Dylan Lucero

I forgot how beautiful it is outside
when I couldn't be bothered,
and I'm lost in what I call home
despite your constant honesty.
Nothing gets through to me.

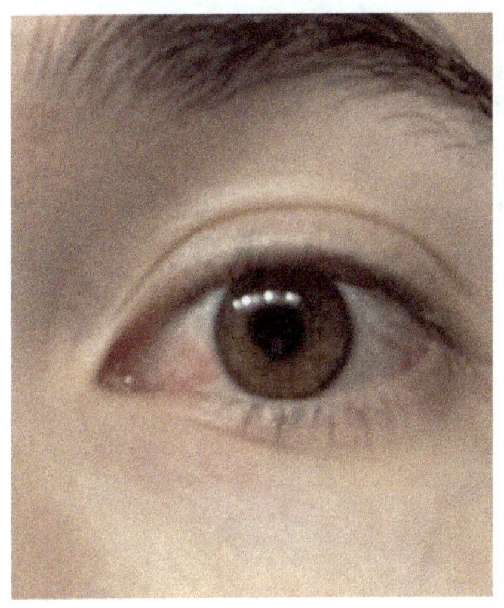

I don't know what I'm looking for,
but I know exactly where it is

There's nothing left to find
Nothing inside these parallel lines

On a road I'm meant to go
inside a car that doesn't start

I can't move the mirrors
or bring myself to think

and the clay can't mold
drying in the lamplight

mend
me

5 Dylan Lucero

You better cancel your plans
fold them up, save them for another day
All we had was buried deep beneath the sand
I've felt it in every word you say
about the country, about this town
When I tried to speak my truth
I couldn't make a sound,
and I think I'm too afraid to move

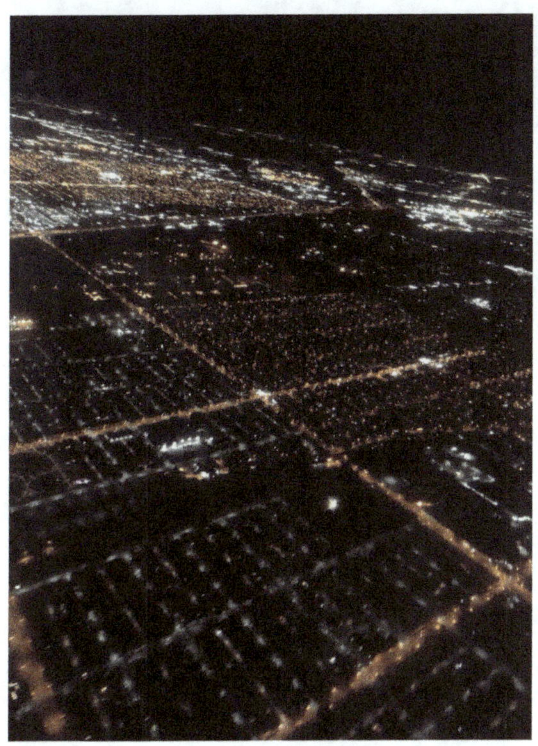

They don't grow grass like they used to,
and days keep passing like hours.
I'm getting further from me with age.

It's funny how we attach ourselves
to these little bits of land–
places that were never ours.

7 Dylan Lucero

Sometimes I dream of that
A life that no one can have

Cold like a dungeon
I'm chained up to you
with nothing more to do

I always do fine in the dark,
so leave me to embark
find a place where I can live
Anything to make me like a kid

I finally let you go,
or rather,
you broke free of me

and when my broken hands
couldn’t find yours
I fell harder than before

and now the warmth,
the beauty,
rests upon my cheeks
as quickly as it leaves

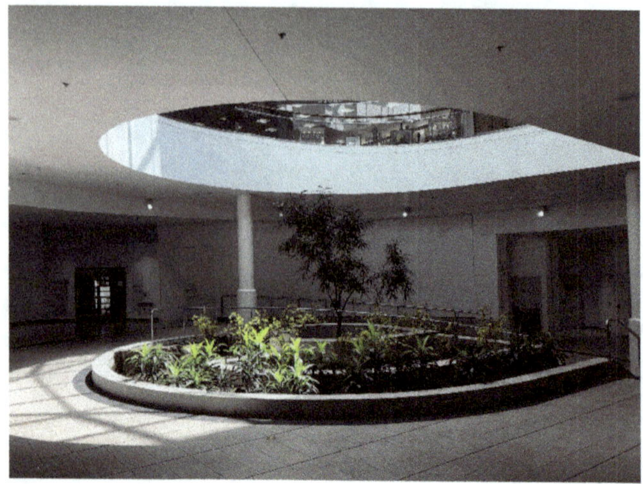

Nothing headlines
and the nights begin to blur
The calendar is left blank
in an era of filler

Monday is Friday
and Wednesday is Sunday
Time has never felt real,
but it owns us anyway

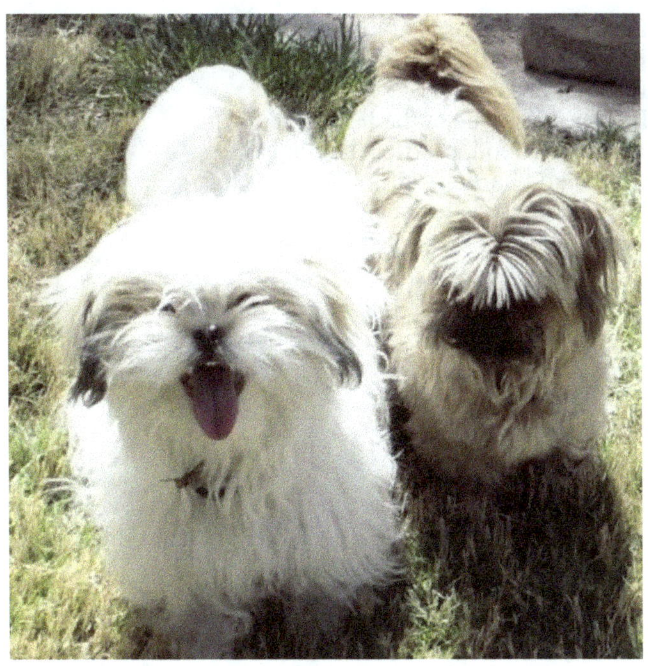

Every breath is precious,
and I couldn't spend another minute
pretending that mine is yours.
Please find your way home.

11 Dylan Lucero

Born into the thorns of marigolds
Forsaken was their name
Haunted by a mirror
Bloodied—rid me of the headspace
Tall as redwood, prettier than light
Grown and hardened into bone
It's yours I chose to warm

No set of words
will ever get my thoughts across
break these looming language barriers

Still, I'll spend all of my money
every second of relief
hoping that you'll humor me
find the patience for me

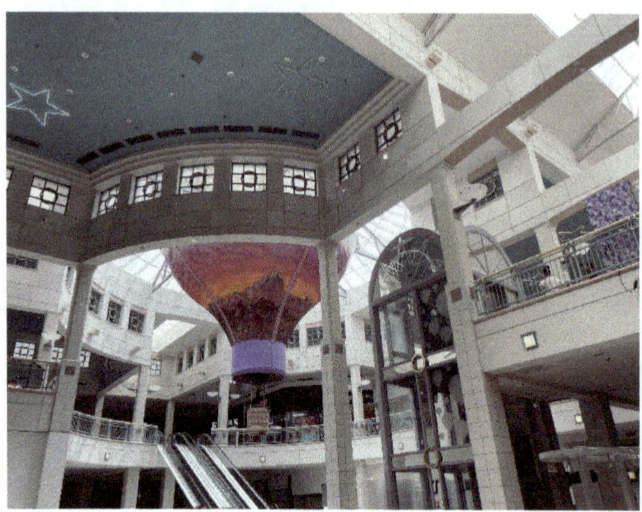

Like true partners in crime
my straightened back to yours
I'll tell you a thousand times
how you cause the time to fly

You were never dull to me.
I can't put it into the words I write,
but for you, I will sure as hell try.

Laughing through the pain
like it's any other day
I can see all of the good in life—
nothing but good in tired eyes

Soul so soft, but safeguarded with steel
Nothing that your smile can't heal,
and through perseverance like no other,
no one is tougher than my mother.

The driven man in me,
he used to drive for me.
We used to tour the country
from New York to Florida
to the train tracks of Iowa.

Took me from school
to the shopping mall
to the publishing house
just down the block.

He's long gone now,
or, perhaps, he was never there at all.

Now there's just tire marks outside
and, somehow, fog inside my room.
I can't drive my car.
It wasn't me–he left with the engine.
He left with my attention.

Think of the thousands of ideas
I'd've loved to share with him
if I wasn't checking the locks on the doors
a hundred thousand times over.
Dead or alive,
he'll never make it home.

I'd choose you over the world
and the places within it.
Dramatic as that sounds,
they're the damning reason
we're apart to begin with.

To be homesick is to yearn for a place you've lost to change. It's when the town you were once molded by is shrinking in the rearview and you can only remember those little glimpses of it. No matter how prepared you thought you were to leave, it turns out you could never be. You never could've imagined the ways in which it would begin to haunt you. In your sleep, in the car, in the middle of a busy store. Even your happiest memories will begin to turn blue. They say you can take a piece of home with you, but that's where my problem lies. Why settle for the crumbs of something that once was whole? I want my youth back. I want my innocence back. I want to take back everyone and everything I've been missing. I want to go home.

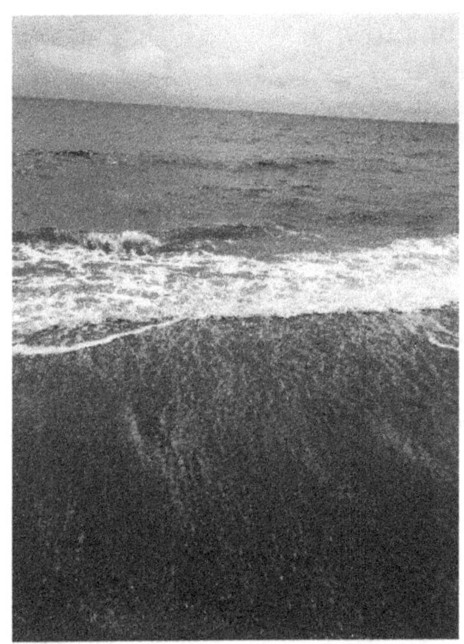

Code red
What used to be blue
has never been this gray

More pressure applied
with every passing day

Every bottle of tea,
every beach I've ever seen,
but at least my hands are clean
...or at least that's how they seemed.

What's one more car on the road?
What's but a scrap of debris?
Alas, some days I forget
there are eight billion of me
tipping dominoes into the sea.

19 Dylan Lucero

I might as well sleep in the snow,
for every night I sleep alone
is worse than sleeping in the cold.

Some days feel okay,
some days feel like doomsday

Road trips, in love with long car rides,
but not when I'm the one to drive.
Your car is fine,
but inside of mine,
I drive like my life is on the line.

Birthdays, holidays, prom night
This should be the time of my life,
but there's people swarming in my mind.
I am a hive, and all I want
is to hide.

Will they be cruel,
will they be kind?
Waiting for the touch,
waiting to be judged,
waiting to be thrown on stage
in front of everyone

Graduation, a complicated feeling
Love to be loved, hate to be seen
An everyday people-pleaser
dying to be believed

I only want them to see
the best version of me,
but I'm bound to run out of masks
not today, not tomorrow, but eventually.

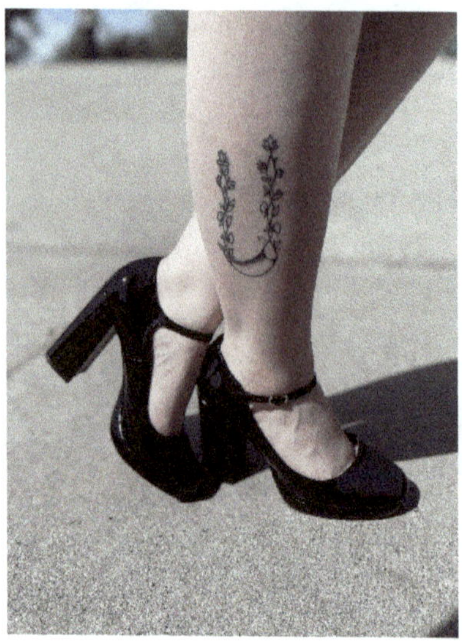

An energy amidst a disastrous storm
Walking in black high heels, wet grass, empty houses
Her smile is tired and her knees are scraped
Still, she looks seamless to me.

Overgrown and raised by rain,
raised by pain, born in weeds
Her eyes: green, glossy, wet
like a pond full of leaves.

She reached up, raised her hands into the clouds
and then they met my softened lips.
They looked like sunlight
and felt like the sky.
She is bound by nature,
or rather,
nature is bound by her.

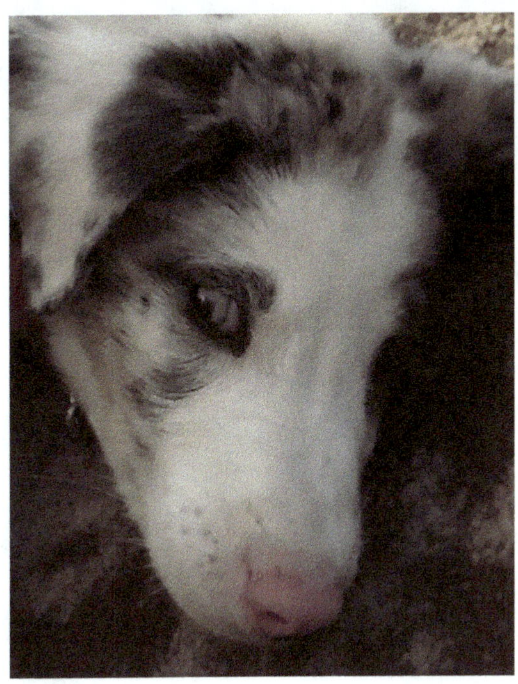

Thoughts run free as you watch,
eyes fierce and curious

They couldn't leave me
Mine, they couldn't leave you

You have my attention
undivided and eternal

23 Dylan Lucero

Blue screen

You’ve got everything you need

Blue screen

Everything

Everything you could possibly need

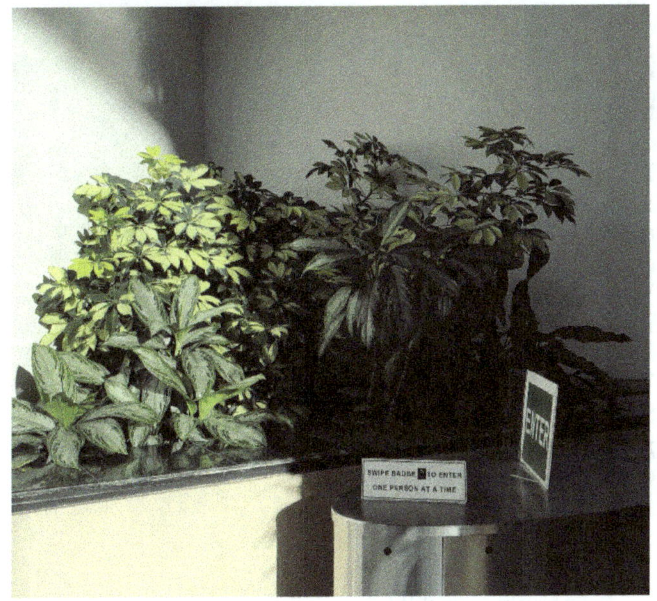

We've all been robbed
not just of money,
but of each of the things
we haven't had the time
nor the courage
to be.

Rorschach
take it back
What does it mean
the scene before me?

Inkblots are the test
I doubt I'll ever rest
again

We will never be romance
As if we had the chance

Rorschach, I beg
Simply tell me
is this mere jealousy,
or a genuine worry?
I doubt it would ever be that easy

There's nothing about love
my eyes could ever tell me

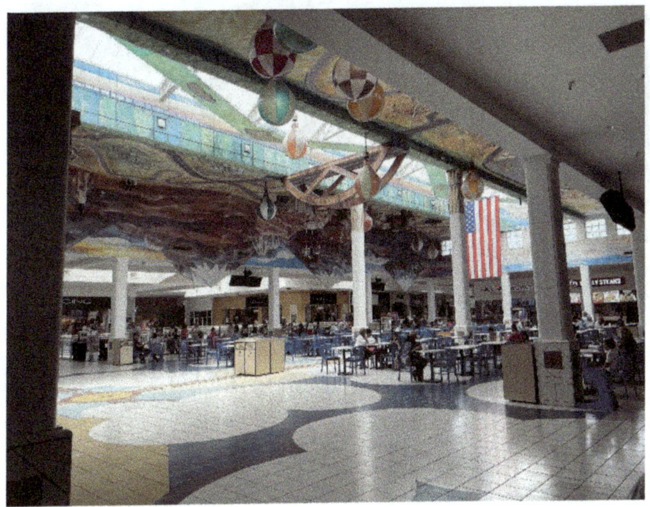

I still know the feeling
the diorama on the ceiling
Since I put that place to rest
I've felt its spirit in my chest

There's less to recognize these days
Home was once all over the place
Now I haven't got room in my head
for anything besides a twin size bed

The moment you open the door
I can see it in the floor
What was once my stomping ground
has turned into a lost and found

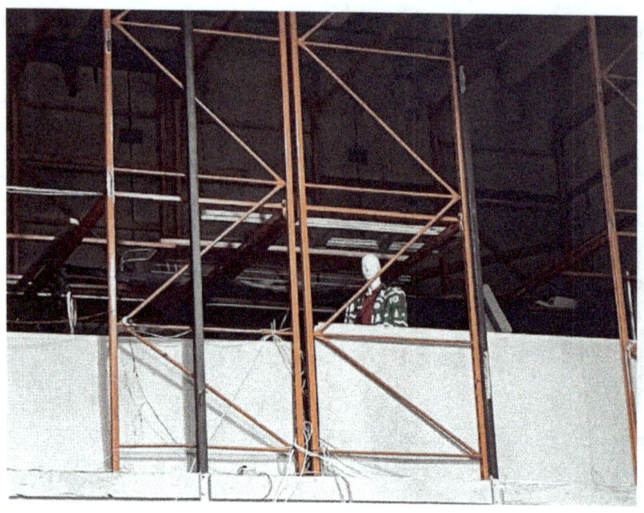

Another day wasted and lost
trying not to look at the clock

Oops, I just checked the time
It's only 4:39

I don't want to work
I just want to live
I've counted down the last few minutes
for the last few hours
wishing I could shower

Oops, I just checked the time again
It's only 4:27

Oh, opportunity
Opportunity in my bones

They're throwing me a bone
and told me all is well.
I have everything here,
but I can't reach it now.

It all sits nocturnal,
gone by the morning.
It will never end.

Dear opportunity,
Opportunity leaves
like leaves from the trees
falling every autumn.

I've found a hole in my brain
and a heart that's always hungry

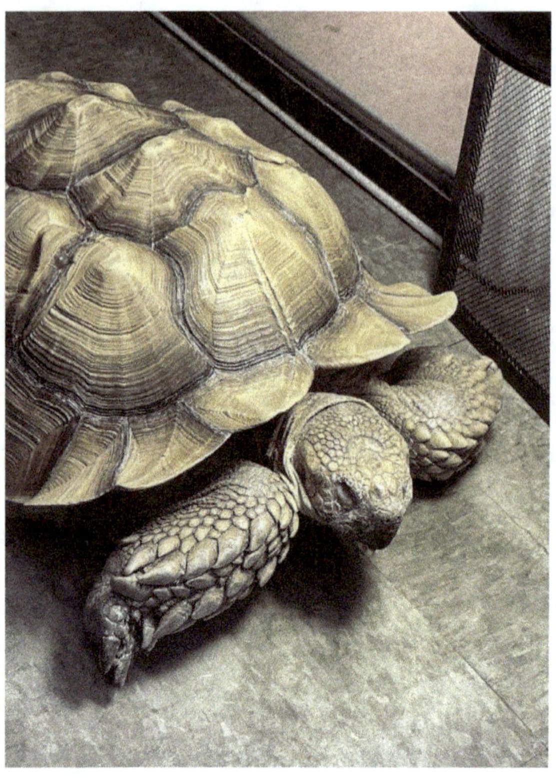

I have passion,
I have will,
but not a single bone in my body
strong enough to climb a hill.

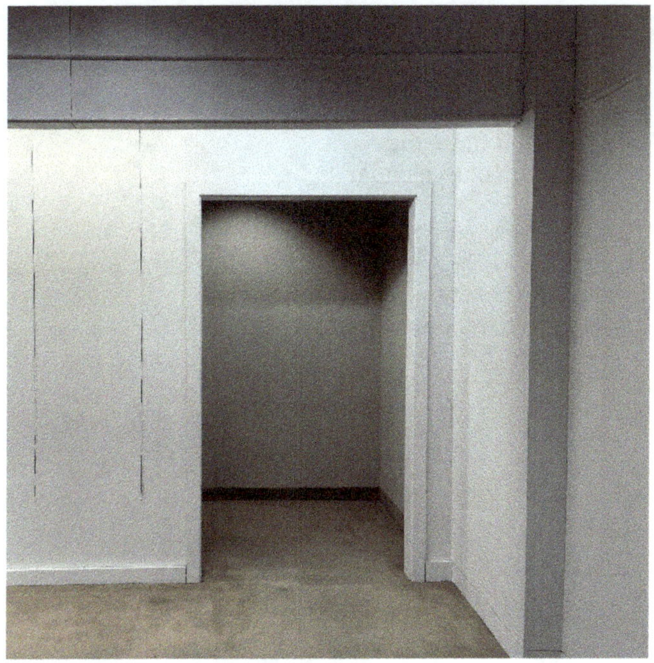

People are nothing but a foot out the door
ready to leave, ready to run free,
but doomed to make ends meet
knowing that they could be something more.

Your touch is a leap year
coming every so often,
and everytime it does,
it must be cherished
like a little bit more time
on the month of a calendar.

Once the dream is over,
I wait an extra day,
I wait these next few Februaries
hoping you may come my way.

Old white shoes and an attitude
Sugar in your eyes, honey on your tongue
There's hesitance written on your lips
Crazy talk coated in red lipgloss
You wrapped me up in candy floss
So much distance, so much silence
was too much on the heart

Had I known from the start
that a room this empty
would be this suffocating
I'd have never had these sweets
if you never would with me
'Cause now I've got some crooked teeth
and you never see them,
but can't you see them
every time I'm smiling?

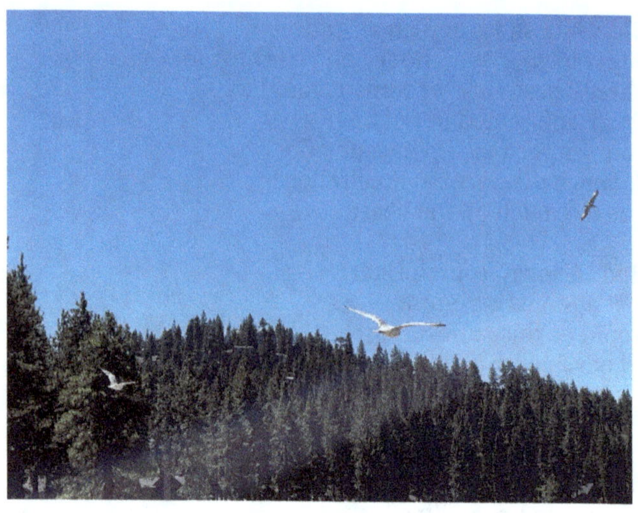

We would finally set sail
if I could just untie the knots
tighter than anything
clustered up along the cable
sinking me into the ocean
only tightened in their sweet time

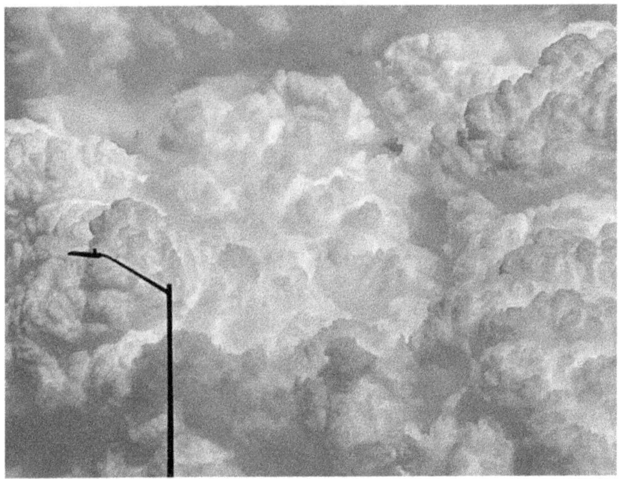

I heard you speak,
but not what you said

Responding reluctantly
Everything gets in, but nothing sticks

Thought is slim every day that I live,
and the more I do amounts to less
waking with an anvil at my chest

Starting the day with static in my brain
tuned out with music, ten songs on repeat
drowning out the bees living inside of me

I just wish I worked a little smarter,
worked a little harder,
for my thoughts could last much longer
if not for a head growing hotter.

35 Dylan Lucero

There’s never enough of you,
and can you even blame me?
Me, the desert
You, the storm clouds
I beg for glorious rain
the longest you will allow
amidst the heaviest drought

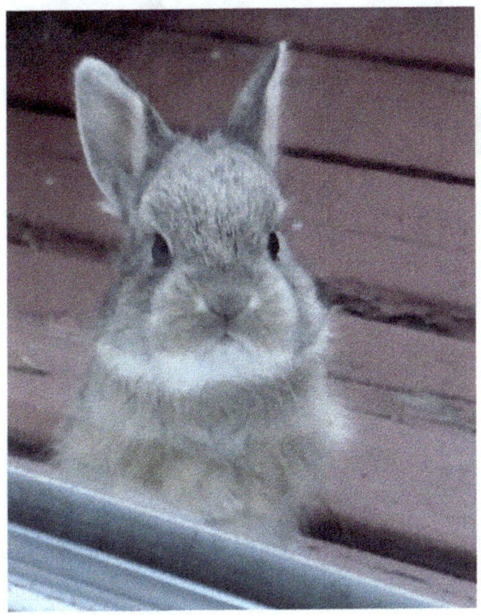

On a sleepless night
I count stars in a darkened sky.

Miles are my lightyears,
and every step not taken towards you
is eighteen thousand laps around the moon.

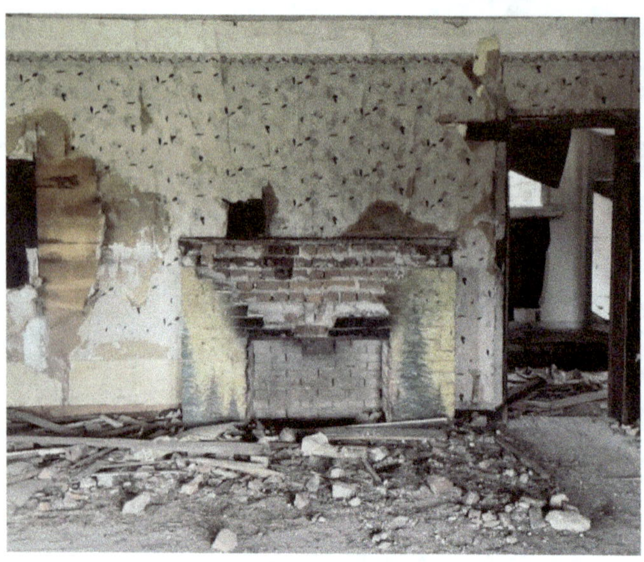

The key doesn't fit
in the places I was raised

What's mine is yours,
and what's yours isn't mine
anymore

Is your house a house,
or is it a home?

Some will say it's needy
maybe even greedy
how I want things to be

but what I wouldn't give
for your blessed name
written all over me

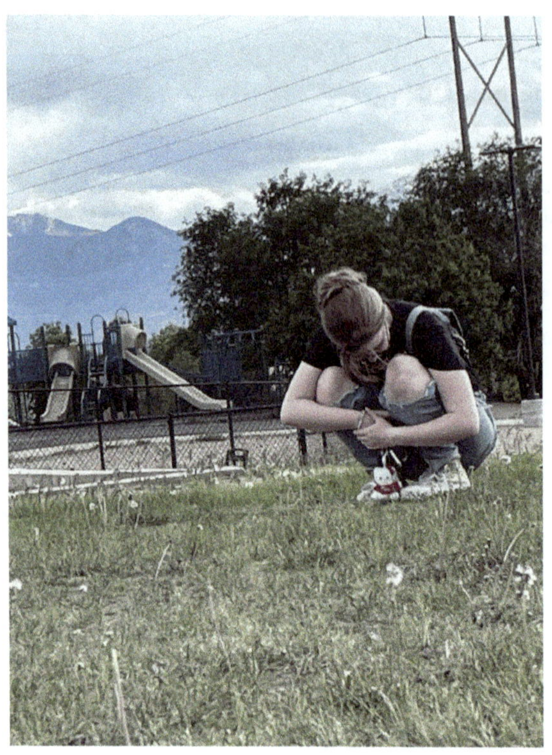

Stickers and temporary tattoos
fake nails and friendship bracelets
pizzas and dinosaur nuggets

You are of the simplest things,
and everything you do
reminds me of youth

It makes its way to you
Give it a day and it's through
Sometimes it's months
Sometimes it's years

You can't tally the pain
or pinpoint an arrival date

All you can do
is wait

This room gets larger
every day
No reason to leave it,
and I'm stuck inside
with windows jammed
the door locked from outside

I write my heart out
sitting in the dark
with a light kept dim
here at the very least
until I may break myself free

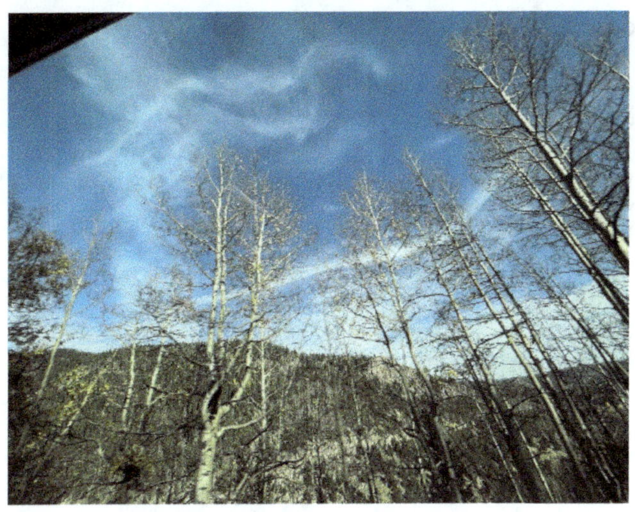

If I could put you up
for the entire world to see,
oh, how we'd burn in the contrast
of everything you've claimed to be

You are a monstrosity.

Your negative energy
is too much for me
It's always what they've done wrong
nit-picking their flaws

I wonder if you speak
the same way about me
when I'm not there to hear
your vents with open ears

Today you finally made me leave.
I hope you're fucking happy.

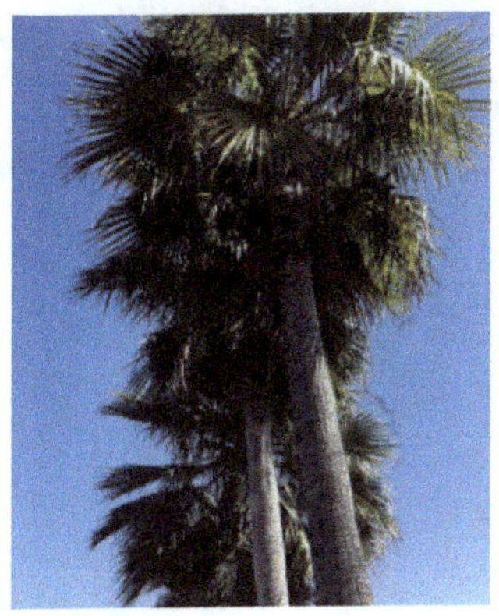

I miss the summer heat
touching the skin of my knees,
the ease of the breeze
flowing through the trees

I miss the smell of summer nights,
the fireworks of early July,
the freedom of a tank top,
the refreshment of an ice pop

I miss the rain hitting the ground
and the grayness of the clouds
I would watch from inside
with a fan blowing closeby

I miss being on the road
never knowing where we'd go
passing all the farmland
with a camera in my hand

Soon the snow will run
from the heat of the sun,
and I'll run out in the daylight
breathing the heaviest sigh

My bored face
in an old place

I've had my fill
with things so nice,
but I need some thrill
I need some spice

It hides behind the window,
it slips past the blinds,
but it's somewhere I couldn't go
even if I tried

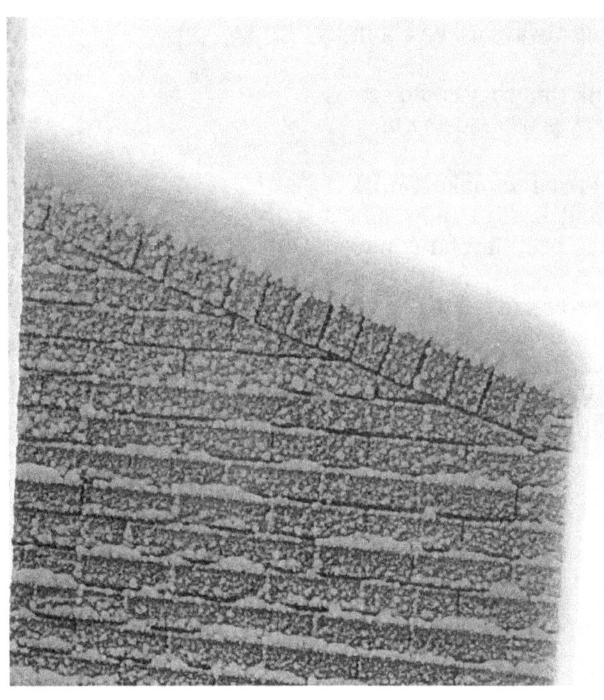

You had me
seeking thrills in the safest places
daring your truth, bringing out lies
holding you in ways you'd rather live without

My warmth always seemed so cold

People always asked about us

I think that they could see
your eyes were losing me

and I tried to make it work
when little did I know, all along
we had been far, far gone

We never sang along,
but the melody kept on
for what felt like forever
and ever and ever and ever and ever and...

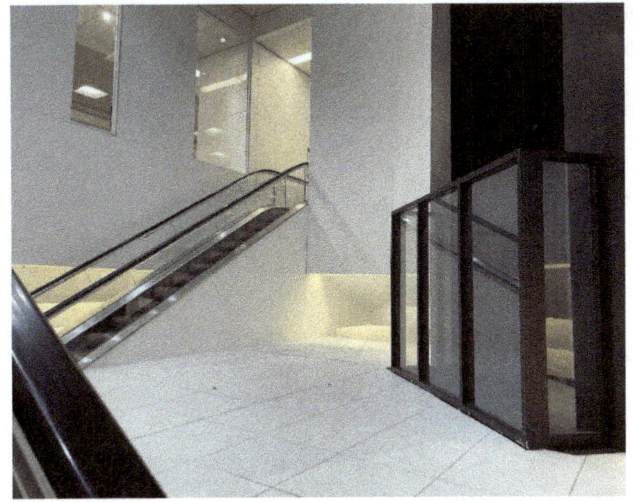

At night I think of all the beds
I'll never get to sleep in again,
and the sound of the mourning dove
as it echoes in my head

The havens in which I was raised
are nothing more than buildings now

I feel hopelessly restless
I feel restlessly hopeless

There's no room for breaks,
for I tend to finish late,
procrastinate,
push my problems to another day

Some days I forget to get up and eat
Some nights I forget to lie down and sleep

Some folks would say I'm not listening,
so please forgive me
if I ask you to repeat
every word you speak.

And lately the air is getting thick
I think my lungs are closing in
It's getting harder to be present
the way this muddy mind has been,
and the walls I built are closing in,
for I'm getting to be

far

too

distant

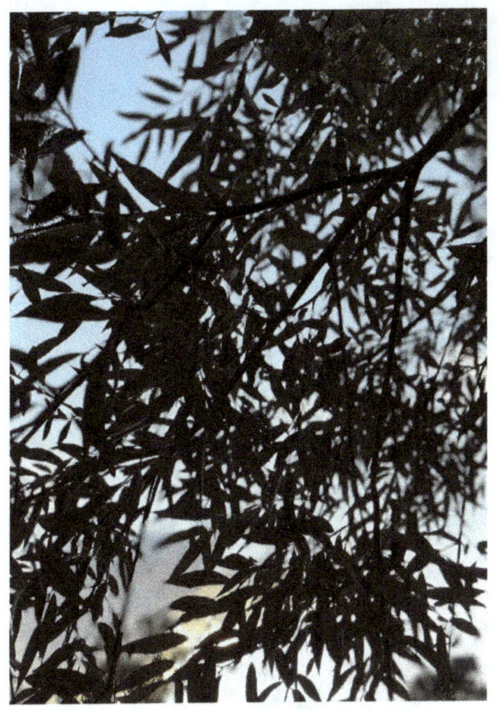

We never really grow up
if we never let it leave
or slip from our grip,
so I hold happiness
close to my heart,
tie myself to a tree,
and try to catch its leaves

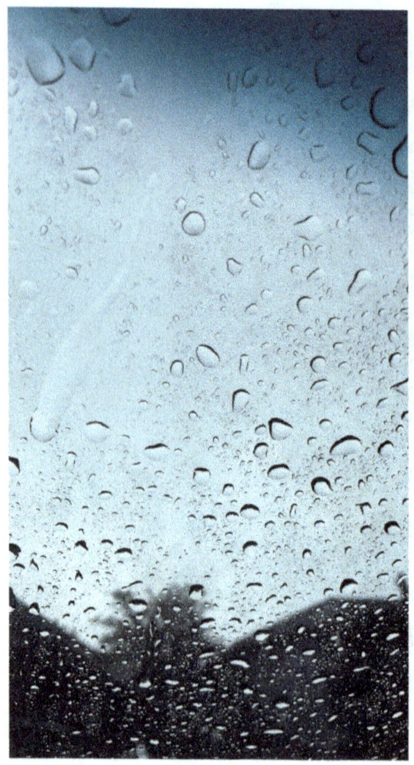

You say not to worry,
"It's all in your head."
"Go play a sport."
Dear me, of course!
We should've done this ages ago.
Why didn't we think of it before?
These useless words have just cured us all!

It feels so nice,
but has it ever felt as right?

The doubts count like sheep
late into the night

I think this feels like you,
but my heart says otherwise

I can feel her warmth
from nobody's but mine

Many say it's there
the faith they've put in me,
but when you live in doubt
the truth is never guaranteed

I wouldn't wish that
on God's worst men,
but what I wouldn't give
for them to understand

Words turned into knives
tossed amongst a pile
so when I turn up old lies
I can cut them for a while

Everybody trusts me but myself

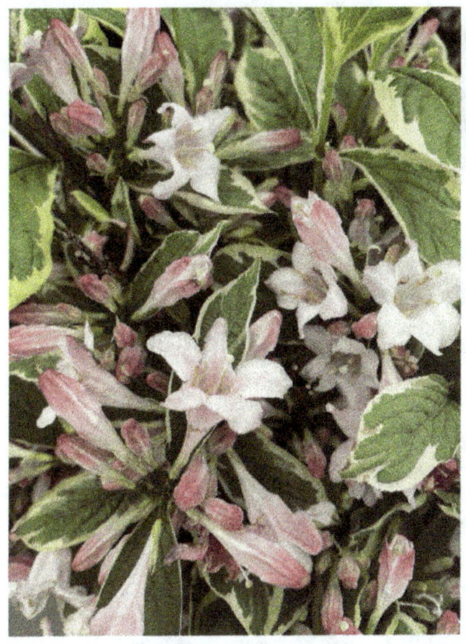

Cuts, bruises, bandages
Burned by daylight
You'll admit to bloodshed
but deny your strength

You say it's sour, but now it's sweet
A sensation still sitting on my tongue
Now that you're gone, I want it all
Damaged yet warm on my skin

Everything is a lesson,
and you wear them well
like my garden full of promise
flowers you cannot see

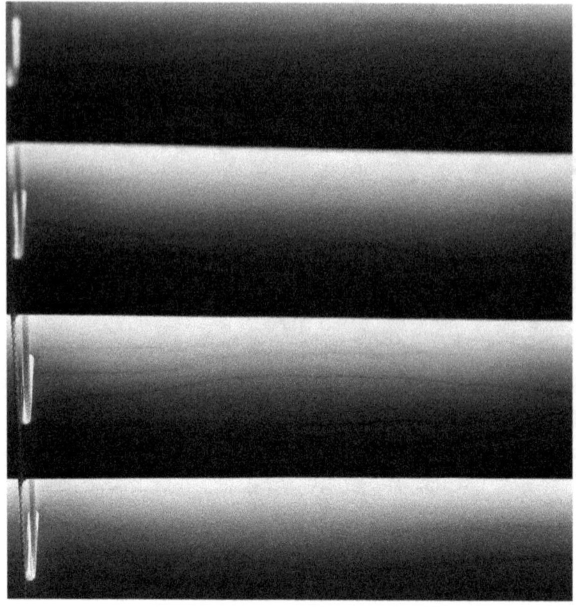

I was made for the stage
but born in a cage
Can't get out, can't get up
and nothing
is heavier
than my blood

Somewhere away from the sun
rests the land of the untouched

That's my favorite place to be
A place that has yet to be seen

Right down to the pores
I pretend that they're yours
I yearn for just one perfect moment
The day that this cycle is broken

You know that I love the sites
The ones that we have lost to time

The bowling alley carpets,
cheese pizzas, chicken nuggets
Sight and scent, that's how we knew them
Kids museums and planetariums,
mini golf and after-parties,
CRTs, cartoons on TV
and field trips to grocery stores
It was tacky, but we weren't bored.

Before everything went and changed
we knew of places that never aged.

And I was there to meet her
Holding hands in the movie theater
I told her that her dress looked nice
I smiled once, and she did twice

Now the kids will grow to eighteen
stuck at home and pressed to screens.
No more peace, no more sites.
Just a hallway with doors shut tight.

How they had their better days
driving their cars, going on dates
when they knew who they were,
why they loved,
where they were and who I am

They must've felt right in their place
They must've had so much fun
before they gave in to the sun

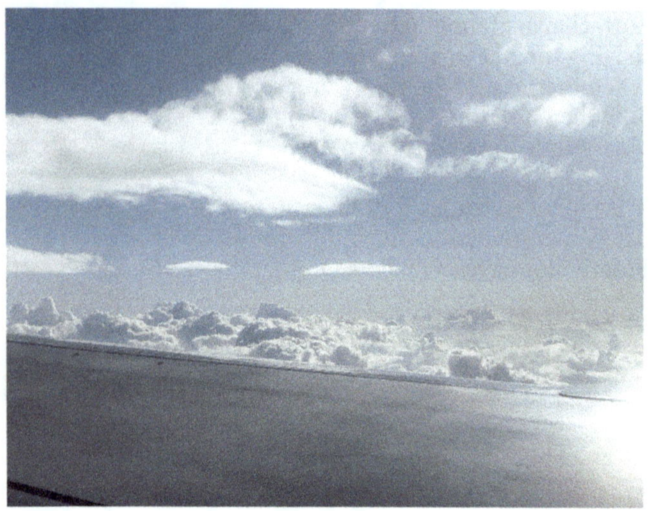

I'm looking for your signs
everywhere the air exists.

I'm losing rest
over what happens next
There's guilt in my bed
and doubts in my head
Anxious, obnoxious, envious
obsessive, hyperactive, inattentive
Another month gone
with every passing day
The urge to quit, to throw it in
because the hardest part
is just trying to live
somewhere in the middle of it

Nobody has a perfect life,
and no two are the same.

The many faces of different places

They all have birthplaces,
but few have a home.

I know a lot about you
how you want to be on someone's mind,
and darling, you deserve to know
lately you've been all over mine.

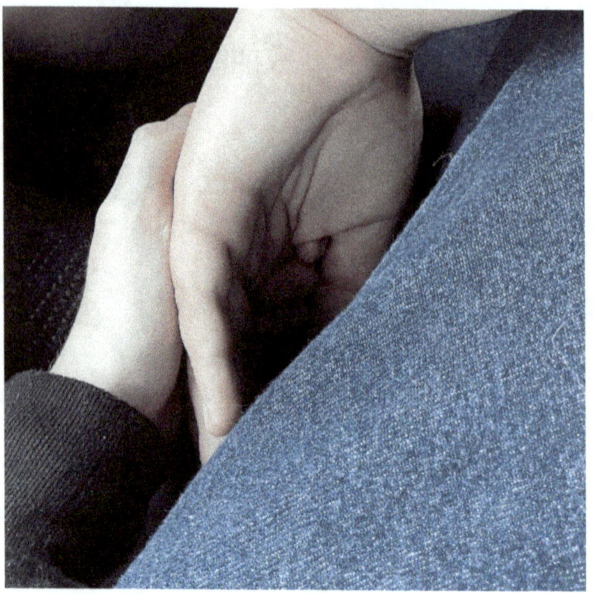

I'll write your name until I break my hand
until nothing more can be said,
and then I'll write with my left
until my fingers turn red

until the blood goes cold
I'd go until they snapped,
but my love, if I did that,
you wouldn't have mine to hold

I'm writing haiku
on touch starved nights like tonight
All of it for you

This world is too big
hard on your gentle smile
You can have my bed

A voice so darling
I wish we shared the same town
They'd sing my heart up

In love and numbness
I'm cursed with a change of heart
You, I never did

I don't sleep much on
nights where you say we should have
tried to already

Balloons above us
Dotted over Sandia
All we need is sun

I've written about
you dozens of times, and I'll
try for thousands more

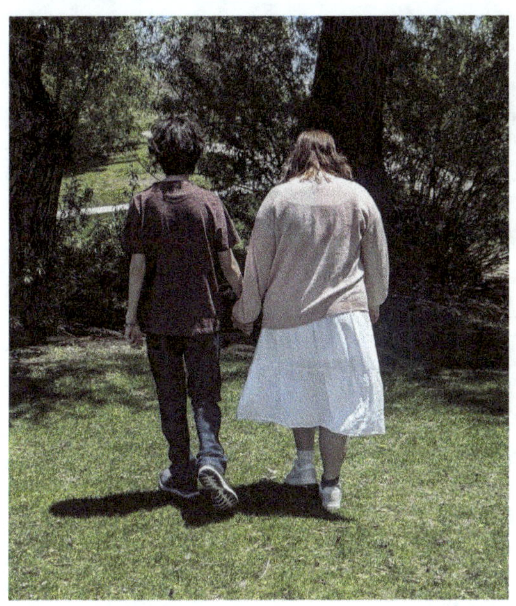

Singing in your bedroom
A ringing in my ear—I hear you
You are in everything,
and the distance will never do
when I just want the sound of you

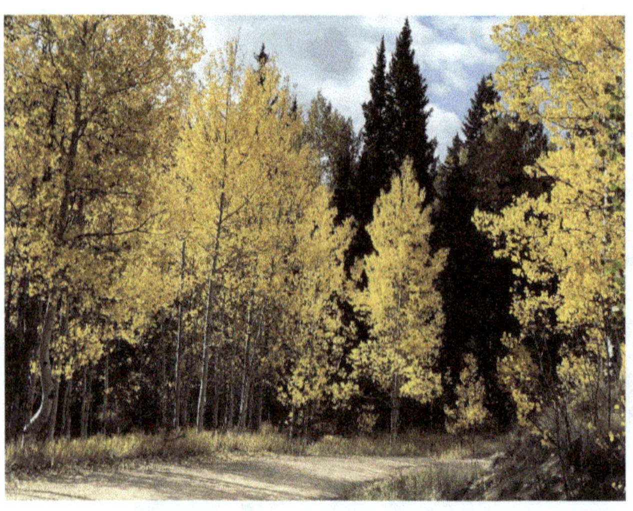

I've lived a hundred different lives
in and out of heaven,
yet I was nothing but miserable
when I wasn't in your presence

A cabin with no heat
I want you,
I need you
like a forest needs its trees

Life would be nothing
if it never got difficult,
for a world without hardship
is a story never told

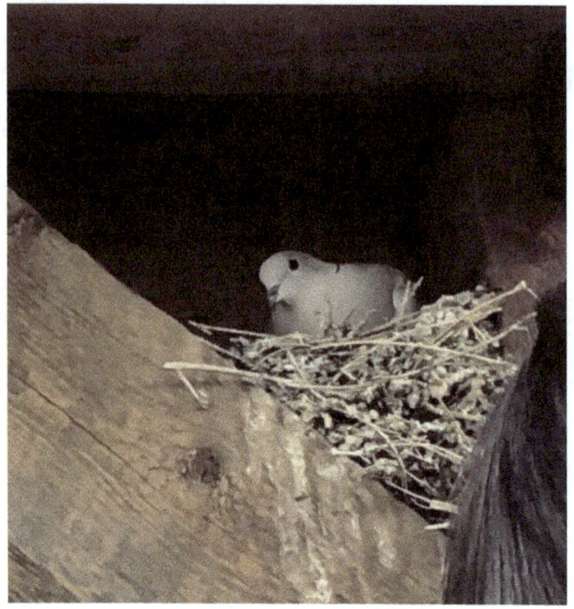

For all that I have
priceless and prominent
every corner of home

in and out the state
near or distant
we've never felt this close,
and here we are now
with everything I could need
I abide boundlessly grateful

An energy that makes strangers smile
You can feel it for miles
She grows some plants, pulls some weeds
in a sun hat on the beach
with a book and some tea

Grown is a family of four,
but your laughter never falls short.
You are loved.
You are incredibly loved.

I get so bored,
so when I get home
I will open the door
and talk to you until four

We can watch movies
laugh at our favorite scenes
I'll be numb in my seat
playing games until three
and you'll be fast asleep
lying next to me

You are my favorite routine

You and me
always taking it slow
Still, you make the raindrops glow

You love my company,
and I cherish yours

I get to know you every day

We met way back when
I was only twelve then
Only then I knew not of myself
Even then you humored me
everything I ever wanted to be

You showed me every book on your shelf

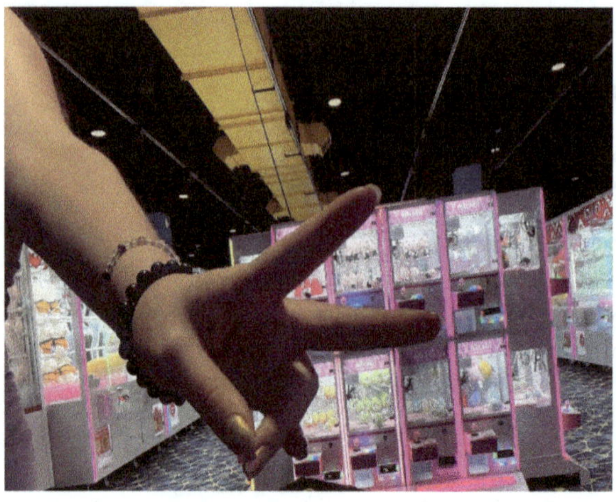

How she knew me from few words
our gaming days and movie nights

And the stupidest things I said
made her laugh the hardest

No one's ever been more charming.

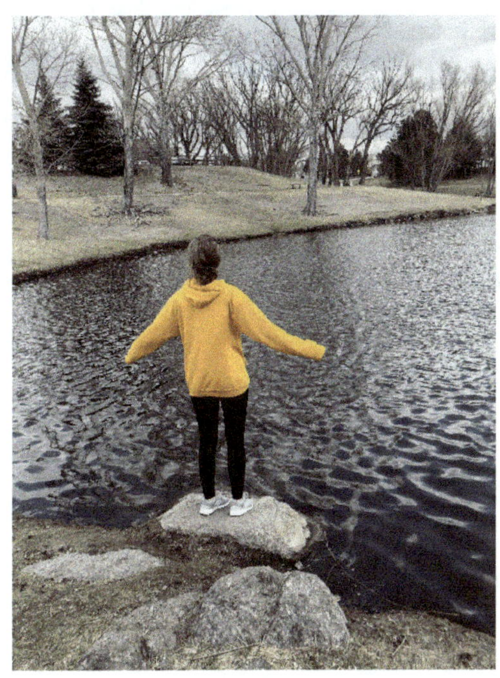

Through and through
she is a majesty
piercing the heavy hail into rain
strolling barefoot on my heart

So full of fun and colored thought
speaking of a sign of angels
her voice wandering into mine
turning my mind into her gaping forest

Through something insuperable
threats to our very livelihood
she is a majesty
the blessing of a lifetime

Your cheeks are kissed by confetti,
and you smile like you're made of sky.
I could see into hours of you
just through a brief glance.

Riding horseback on dinosaurs
lassoing everything in your way
boots have become a part of you
like the feeling of grass beneath your soles

You seem just like the glow of Saturn.
It's the best way I can describe
the look that was in your eyes
when I woke up by your side.

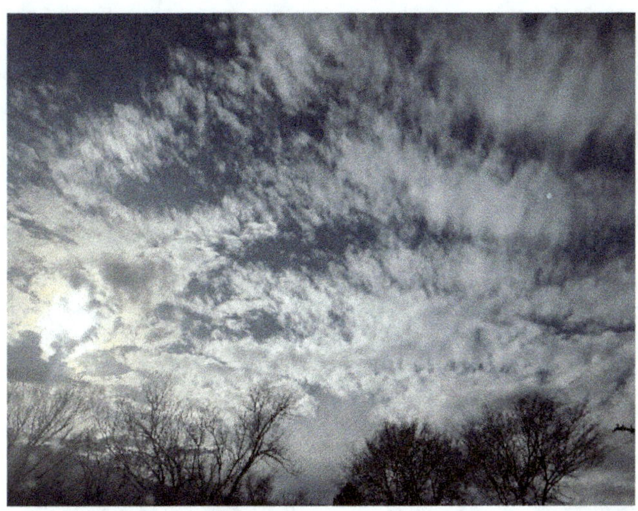

The future is now,
or so they claimed it'd be.
There's no flying cars or time machines.
Instead, there's oceans full of batteries.

And if we had the technology
I'd reach through the screen
and pull you over to me
just before this country sinks.

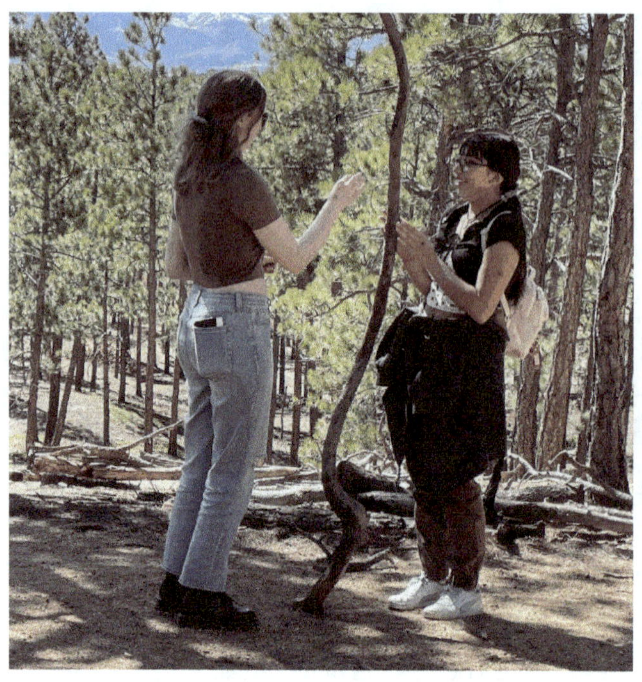

You are my bucket list.

It doesn't matter how I spend my life
so long as you're in it.

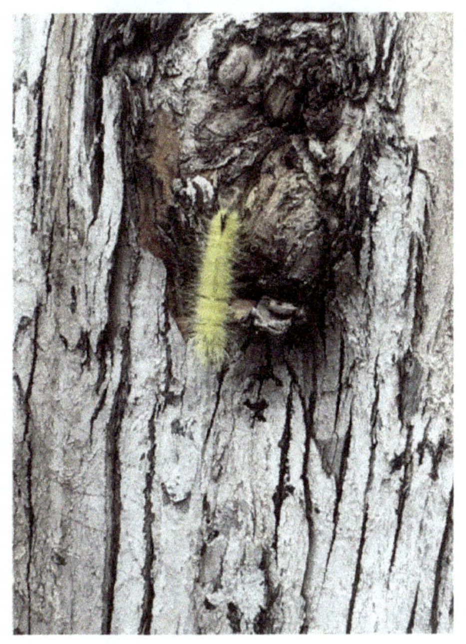

I am growing
but one tree
out in the wild
down beneath the ground.

I grow mine
with water and some sun.
You grow yours
with oil and some fire.

There is pain in your story
It wasn't all just glory

All that you want to hide
it makes me want to cry,
but you should always know
that I will hold onto your heart
through the day that I die

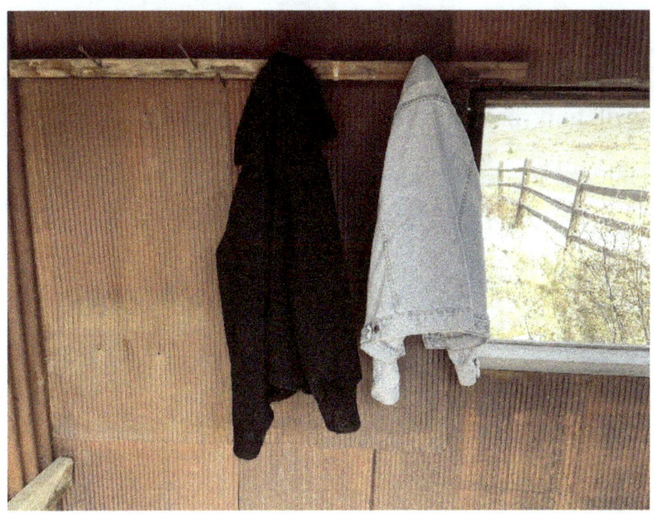

You always cover pricey meals
always hold in how you feel
Your shoes are closed-toed and made of steel
and you're all bruised up from arch to heel

For you always stand, but never sit
You never take, but always give
This is the life you've always lived
One with closed, doubt-plastered lips

Like you have something to prove
Like I'd hate you for telling the truth
But you–you deserve some loving too.
I love you, and your simple honesty will do.

83 Dylan Lucero

A day of perfect rain
has yet to come my way,
but in the quieter hours
I will find you some flowers.

Only the loudest and brightest will do
The ones that remind me of you

Looking like this is the truth
Mountains are not to be moved
There's nothing for me to prove
no matter what I do

Some things stay tragic,
for my hands were never magic,
and some answers stay suggestions
in a sea so full of questions

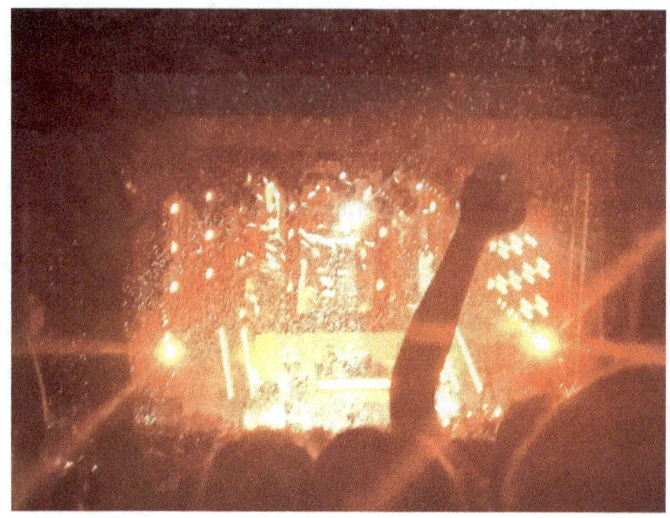

Eight billion people
and you're the one I picked.
I've met plenty of faces,
but not a soul like yours
for as long as I have lived.

My ankles finally broke,
but once I'm fine to go
I'll meet your pretty face
anyplace,
anywhere we want to go

We know what we want now
running from these little towns
One day I'll pick you up,
carry you around,
take you to any city

And you're lovely as you are
Your voice is made of stars,
and there's valleys in your heart

I'd pick you over anyone,
any stranger in this city

any city

Everybody has too much to say
My insecurities, my face, my weight

They will tell me
it's confidence I need,
but all I need is silence.
All I need
is to breathe.

A simple vessel
inside you will find
a beating heart,
an open mind,
the unexplored,
my magnum opus

I am untouched,
I am vacant
I am a cove,
I am an ocean

My arms, my legs, my lips
never had a say in this
It's only my skin
It's all that it is.

You are a daily medicine
I can only handle you in small doses
I'm sorry I can't be your twenty-four-seven

A second
minute
hour
day
week
month
year
decade
century
millennium
eternity

No matter how long it takes
you are so worth the wait.

I found a house for sale
It's been vacant for a while
I'm not sure it's one you'd like,
but I can show you inside.

The walls still hold up well
We'll tear some down if we have to
We'll line the ones we kept up
with photos of the two of us.

The living room is warmly lit
like one you'd find in a mansion,
or, if you grew up like me,
a warm, cozy adobe.

The kitchen is nice and open
Lots of cupboards, lots of counter space
Perfect for pasta, perfect for cake,
perfect for late-night milkshakes.

The bedroom is important
It's where we'll spend nights in,
and under a hundred blankets
is where we'll be lying.

It's not the cleanest house
There are cracks in the showers
Yes, it's been lived in before,
but we can make this one ours.

If you're just like me
born to the start of the century
each day had teemed
with soft, pleasant dreams,
scattered hot air balloons,
bounce house-filled rooms,
fruit snacks and granola bars,
video games and playing cards,
the turn of an elementary school hall,
the food court of a dying mall

As I see these things go
I realize no one will know
precisely how they look inside
this growing mind of mine
colored in white and blue and pink,
yellow and red and aquamarine

Nobody born in this century
ever came to see
the same light as me

It's never been this easy
taking the time to sleep,
so I tend to stay up late.
I sleep right through the day.

A library
full of books I'll never read
My parents' first fortune
and they gave it all to me.
I've never been this thankful,
this grateful,
so I'll wash the dishes when I'm able.

Then in the night
I found a faraway lover,
the kind I don't deserve
like the warmth of the summer

Miracles
It's never been this easy to live,
so for everyone I know
all I want is to give.

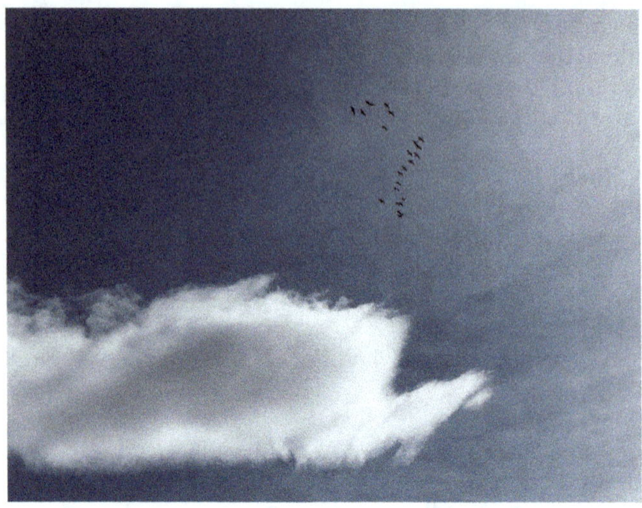

That's just what everybody wants
Something more than what they've got

But I try to count my blessings
It's the blessings that count

Whether I made it outside
or I slept in at home,

I'm a cherished friend
or a text on a phone,

the robots replaced me
or the printing grew old,

or I've been put to rest,
please don't cry alone.

To Earth itself, I plead,
make my hope their own.

My kin,
my reasons to live,

my kids,
my grandkids,

if I'm no longer here,
just let my word be known.

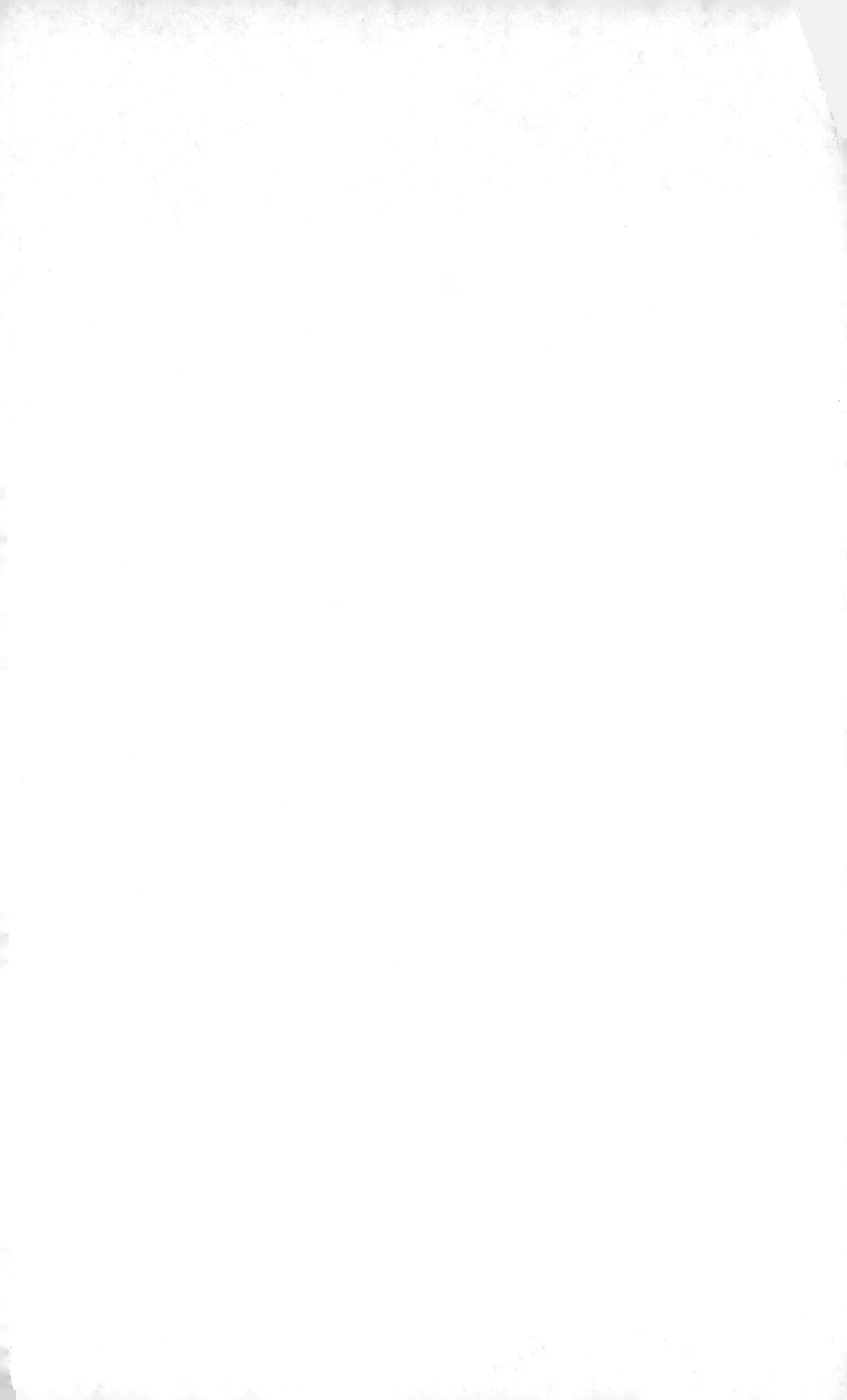

www.ingramcontent.com/pod-product-compliance
Lightning Source LLC
LaVergne TN
LVHW020512100826
845148LV00003B/767

9798218574420